The Forest For The Trees

Dear Cindy,
You are so intuitive about life —
May these poems resonate with
your conclusions...

Mimi Pantelides

Mimi Pantelides

THE FOREST FOR THE TREES

MIMI PANTELIDES

THE FOREST FOR THE TREES by Mimi Pantelides, © Copyright 2021, Mimi Pantelides. All Rights Reserved and Preserved. No part of this book may be reproduced or transmitted in any form or by any means, electronic or mechanical, including photocopying, recording, or by information storage and retrieval systems, without written permission of the Publisher with exceptions as to brief quotes, references, articles, reviews, and certain other noncommercial uses permitted by copyright law.

For Permission requests, write to:

YBR Publishing, LLC
PO Box 4904
Beaufort SC 29903-4904
contact@ybrpub.com
843-900-0859

THE FOREST FOR THE TREES

MIMI PANTELIDES

ISBN-13: 978-1-7349515-6-1

YBR PUBLISHING, LLC

Jack Gannon – Co-Owner, Production Manager
Cyndi Williams-Barnier – Co-Owner, Production Editor
Bill Barnier – Co-Owner, Senior Editor
Loreen Ridge-Husum – Art Director
Michelle Owens – Marketing Agent

THE FOREST FOR THE TREES

You cannot see the wood for trees. Continued proverbial, being found in an anti-popish tract of the reign of Charles II.

*From him who sees no wood for trees
And yet is busy as the bees
From him that's settled on his lees
And speaketh not without his fees,
Libera nos.*

A Letany for S. triers, 1682
The Proverbes of John Heywood, 1546

THE FOREST FOR THE TREES

MIMI PANTELIDES

ACKNOWLEDGMENTS

Thanks go to Bobby King who worked tirelessly to work and rework the recordings of each poem, as well as being the bass player, and to Ellen Britton who was so wonderfully positive during the process.

Will Barrow who miraculously was able to create the musical introductions for each piece, thinking with his fingers on the keyboard from one end of musical history to another.

Working with these consummate professionals has given me a glimpse into the world of modern music production. They were kind and patient and good. The experience has been an education in itself.

For YBR Publishing, especially Jack and Cyndi, I am so grateful that y'all have made this process so positive. Today, no matter what we may think or create, without dedicated people to mold it into marketable shape and with their knowledge and experience to push it out of the nest, a book will only ever be a lost file on a laptop or a few sheets pressed in a notebook.

Thank you.

THE FOREST FOR THE TREES

MIMI PANTELIDES

My mother wanted her only daughter to be a child of nature. When I was young, I didn't believe it was important. From the distance of a few decades, my opinions have changed somewhat.

> *After a lifetime of study and concert going,*
> *Museum prowling and critique reading,*
> *I have come to a firm conclusion:*
>
> *The best of art, music and literature,*
> *Springs unexpectedly from*
> *Something noted in the natural world;*
> *Notice it, no matter how small,*
> *Pass it on instead of passing it by,*
> *And suddenly, these small, unnoticed things*
> *Become larger than life;*
> *Gifts more precious than gold.*

...Now, I think my mom was right.

~Mimi

THE FOREST FOR THE TREES

MIMI PANTELIDES

DEDICATION

To all of you, my family both two-footed and four-footed who have taught, encouraged, and surrounded me with love, thank you endlessly. I couldn't be without you. All the creations that have come from me are from you.

This particular volume owes a debt to three friends in particular; three ladies who are writers and poets, and it is their example that convinced me to pursue this project. You are not responsible for the product, only the inspiration! Any lack in the final version is mine alone, but Carolyn Kephart, Annell St, Charles, and Barbara Russell, your books and poems have lit a path for me to follow. Thank you.

THE FOREST FOR THE TREES

MIMI PANTELIDES

FORWARD

"Dear Reader"...

Remember when every book started out with that phrase? We readers were addressed personally, and immediately invited in to participate in the story about to unfold. I would like to invite you to participate in the miniature stories set down in this little volume. Each one began with a little slice of my life, though it may have gained fiction along the way to become a lesson learned.

You can read them and hear them read at the same time if you wish. Just click on the QR Code on each page to hear the poem read out loud.

"You can't see the forest for the trees" is an old proverb referring to an inability to put things in perspective. I hope that as you share these verbal snapshots, you will enjoy a wider perspective and see "the forest" in all its largesse.

THE FOREST FOR THE TREES

MIMI PANTELIDES

Publisher's Note

The poems within these pages all have a QR code beside the title. With a QR Reader app on their phones, readers can scan that code and listen to the author recite the poems as they read along for a fuller multimedia poetic experience.

THE FOREST FOR THE TREES

A BUCK, A CHIPMUNK, AND A TURKEY

Back at the car
Ladies pass loudly,
Their chattering shattering my mood.
Focus... Think... Remember...
What aura rests on my shoulders
Left from my walk in the woods?

Vision, sight and smell, heartbeat
Synchronous with an eight-point buck
With his full and crested neck,
He could kill me in an instant,
But he won't.
It's not in his nature.

Grave and graceful turkey in
Their weighted purposeful dance;
How many were there?
Thirty if there was one,
Linked and comfortable in their
Ages-old path.

THE FOREST FOR THE TREES

And, oh,
I know where lies the chipmunk's
Lair.
He showed it me against his will.
He couldn't help stashing his
Acorn there in case I tried to steal.

Unlike the squirrels endlessly
Burying their bounty,
The chipmunk will eat his when
Winter comes.
The squirrels will only scratch their
Heads wondering how that oak
Tree sprouted in the path where
They think they might remember
Burying some food.

Why do these wordless pictures carry more weight
Than the pictureless words of the ladies?

The answer makes me want to turn back.
Back to the eight-point majesty of the buck,
Whose message is borne through the earth not the air.
The turkey I feel in my walk, not my brain,
The chipmunk who I can love like my children without fear.
I know what he is about, and why,
And where he'll be tomorrow.
But the ladies' words?
Even they don't know
What their words
Will sow.

A NEW YEAR'S WISH 2020
REE-DIK-U-LUS (but true)

I woke up to the phrase, (I thought) quite clear...
"Honey you have a pignon in your ear."
To which I replied with helpless cheer,
"Where? Who? What? A pignon in my ear?!"
Now, the most hilarious of all this year,
Is that I was quite asleep, but surely did hear,
"Honey, you have a pignon in your ear." For a "wake-up"
murmured wish to steer
My groggy brain cells on January One to peer-

At the infant 2020 morning still to appear,
For at 5 a.m., in the dark, I am in low gear;
This new year has begun with a Pagliaccio leer.
In my humblest opinion of the diminutive pignon,
A better repository than one's ear,
Is definitely,
Positively,
Unquestionably,
...Beer.

Still, what a relentlessly funny phrase my dear,
As a first utterance of the fledgling year,
Turn over, whisper liltingly, "Honey, you have a pignon in
your ear."
To which I reply between gasps for air,
"I don't have a pignon in my ear! And,
Don't put pignons in *your* ear, my dear!
Put them in your beer!

NEW YEAR'S WISH, 2020 – PART II
PINIONED

My opinion of the desert pignon
Needs revising, it is clear
For the pignon
Is neither diminutive in size,
Nor shaped to fit a loved one's ear.

It must have been a different term,
For I know now, awake and clear,
The meaning must have been pignoli
Which is small, tasty, slick to feel
And common enough in our household.

More common than the tree we've seen
Growing tenaciously in harsh environs;
Brave enough, to be sure, to merit emulation,
But not as toothsome, cunning sweet,
As the seed from which the conifer grows.

A SURPRISING HUNGER

Years after we last met
Face to face,
Smile to smile,
Voice to voice,

I realized a hunger.
How surprising
To taste the sweetness
From her eyes.

A look welling
From the heart
Pure and cool;
Quenching;

Washing away
The dust of doubts
Left from
Ink on the pages
Of our correspondence.

The music of friendship
Almost losing its way,
Echoing like
Voices down a long
Hallway

THE FOREST FOR THE TREES

Studded with doors
Leading to strangers' lives;
Concrete stairwells
Spiraling down to
Dark corridors –
Closed, cold, dank –

Dry whispers
Suddenly
Brightened, nourished,
Shining with light;

Now warmed and replenished;
Fed from the waters
Of that spring.

It washes soul deep,
That song of connection;
One friend to another;
Clear and bright;

Better than love,
For this carries no burden;
No weight of duty
No debt of promise
Impossible to pay.

In one short afternoon
A hunger
Surprised me
Never realizing
Its existence,

And in one
Full look, one grateful hug,
One shared laugh,
One trembling – almost tear,
The hunger is banished,
Sated,
Retired to its dark
Hidden corner.

As my front door closed
Behind my friend,
The click said,
Well...
That was a surprise!
A hunger
I hadn't realized.

ANOTHER'S PURPOSE

A perfect day!
Thank you, Goldilocks...
For the nursery rhyme:
Not too cold, not too hot;
Not too still, not too fraught.
Perfect sunbeams playing on the leaves,
Taking the deer-coat-color of the forest floor;
Dabbing it gold, yellow, and neon green.
...And so those sunbeams serve.

Silent leaves suddenly find their voice;
Falling, twirling, whispering down,
Settling so lightly on the ground –
Their last song before winter.
...And so, the leaves serve.

The turkey in their majesty,
Their dance of sex...
Their minuet in the compost
Shelters seeds and nuts,
...And so, they too, serve.

Counterpoint to the stately birds,
Flicking tails, chucking, scampering,
Squirrels, busy, busy,
Burying their treasures in the path;
...Unknowingly, they serve;

They'll never find their bounty come spring.
They serve another's purpose,
...Little do they know.
Perhaps we each serve in that way,
...Little do we know.

THE FOREST FOR THE TREES

Alan Earnest Ball

Allen Earnest Ball Died Unexpectedly July 4, 2019

"Allen Earnest Ball died unexpectedly July 4, 2019"...
And he deserves a paean...

Allen Ball.
The wallpaper man...
That is how we met him.
We quickly learned a little of how much more he was.

He was a generous man
Who gave our whole family glasses
So, we could look at the solar eclipse.
AN ASTRONOMER.

His meticulous, perfect cuts
And appreciation for a beautiful paper.
AN ARTIST.

He knew to let the paper "rest"
Once it was "booked".
A WISE MAN.

He admired his wife's drawings,
He told me so, and admired mine;
Was educated,
Had a gentle, dry humor
And arrived on time.
A GENTLEMAN.

THE FOREST FOR THE TREES

I liked him.
We all did.
Sorry he is gone from us.
A RENAISSANCE MAN~
From whom we learned so much.

CHLOROPHYLL AT WORK

Funny where words can lead.
They lead, and my mind follows.
I read them aloud and hear new thoughts.

Consider light.
When the light is right, you can see the air.
It truly is blue, and because it hit me,
I could not walk far today.
New words, new thoughts,
Kept stopping me in my tracks.

When the light is right,
When I see it right,
I can see the light
Penetrating the Ash leaves.

Chlorophyll at work.
I don't really see it, I suppose,
I sort of – know it;
Assume it from third grade science class.

Is it true?
I don't really know,
But I believe it
Though I don't feel it
Not being an Ash tree.

My leaves are small and tough.
They are not translucent and light-edged
As those gracing yonder sapling.

THE FOREST FOR THE TREES

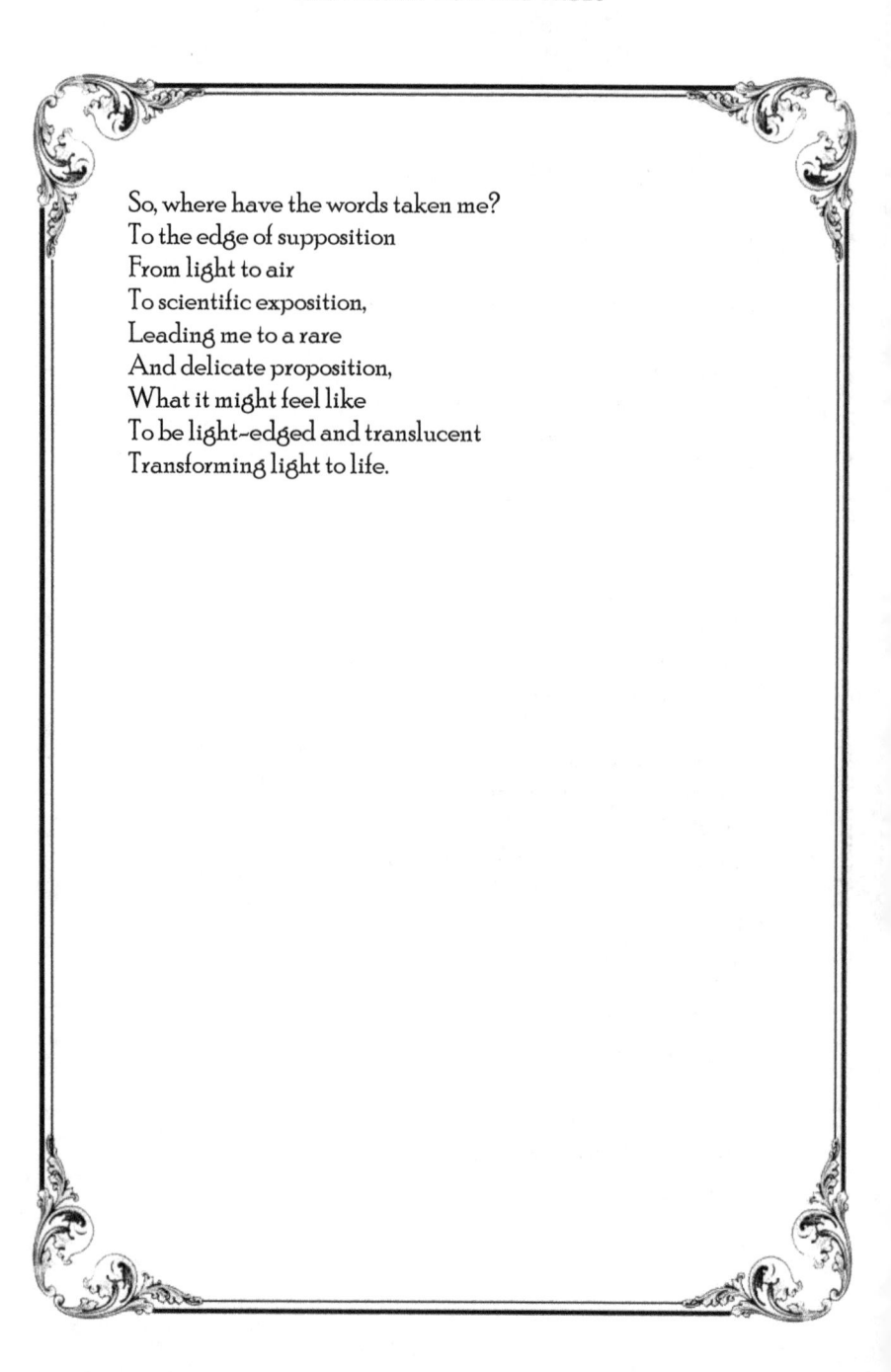

So, where have the words taken me?
To the edge of supposition
From light to air
To scientific exposition,
Leading me to a rare
And delicate proposition,
What it might feel like
To be light-edged and translucent
Transforming light to life.

BEAUTY IN THE EYE OF THE BEHOLDER

I am beautiful because my beloved
Sees me that way.
In me he sees perfection
Mirrored in my eyes;
A spark of acceptance, understanding,
And, yes, love…
What else can it be?
But an outpouring of tenderness,
Sweet humor,
Smiles from the inside out –
It pours both ways
This liquid flow of smiles.
From eyes to lips to heart to ground,
Gone to ground
To the bosom of the earth
Secure in the living heartbeat
That is natural life.
But,
Without him
That beauty turns to ashes;
Words dying on my lips,
Eyes turned inward
Listening to the decay
Of what was once luminous;
Glowing,
Growing and flowing;
That sweet river
Nourishing
The best impulses of human feeling;

THE FOREST FOR THE TREES

Now become
Parched
Dreading the day
As that tender beauty
Dries up
And blows away

So much dust
To add to the desert
Of current events.

BETTER LIFE THROUGH CHEMISTRY

Long ago and far away
I read in my childhood room
With its north facing window
And fireplace on the wall to the east,

That the Indians of the west
Would not sit for photographs
In the belief their souls would be stolen.
From our wise promontory of 1950,
We all chuckled at the absurdity
Of their wisdom.
From the safety of our knowledge,
Our better life through chemistry,
Our higher understanding fed by
Oleo, skim milk, square tomatoes,
DDT, Thalidomide, and political containment,
We mocked the naïve certainty
Of the native people.

Such savages, to worship the earth and air;
Such idiots to anthropomorphize animals;
Such children to believe rocks, earth and water
Contained energy that fed their people.
I think much of that belief still lives;
Somehow underpinning
The soul sick rhetoric-
The dialogue that speaks of skin color
As a defining characteristic.
And it proves the wisdom of
Those native shamans was right as rain.

Allowing those photographs
To be taken by Thomas Easterly
Began the destruction of American souls.
For what is a soul after all?

Soul is common enough lingo
Soul- a legitimate word in our day-to-day discourse.
Scientists have gone to great lengths

To measure the soul of man
Without much great success.

And yet,
Does anyone deny the existence of soul?
The breath of life?
I, for one, can feel my soul.
I know when it expands; when it contracts.
Too late, I realize when it is diminished.
And the reality,
Learned from our natives in the U.S. of the 1800's
Is that we agree to forfeiting our souls.
Soul is not taken away by force,
But by tacit agreement
That we only realize when it is too late.

Oddly, there exists a great divide—
A fundamental difference between the
Representation created by photographs,
By chemical manipulation of light,
And that created by human hands;
By living imagination; the touch guided
By feeling and im-perfection;
Creations borne of personal history;
The stuff of experience and relation
To the subject of art...
Exposure of the artist's soul, if nothing else,
That represents the subject
Through empathic dialogue
Rather than a non judgmental reflection
That by a trick of light can

Misrepresent the whole of a human being.

In that leap away from soulful exchange
Lies the first flight in the death of a soul.
Ironically, the death of one soul,
Hah! Not even death, for that is clean and definite.
Rather the diminishing of one soul drags at the glory of every other.

There is no escape, and worse, when shown the way out,
In these brilliant times,

Most prefer imprisonment.

BIRDSONG

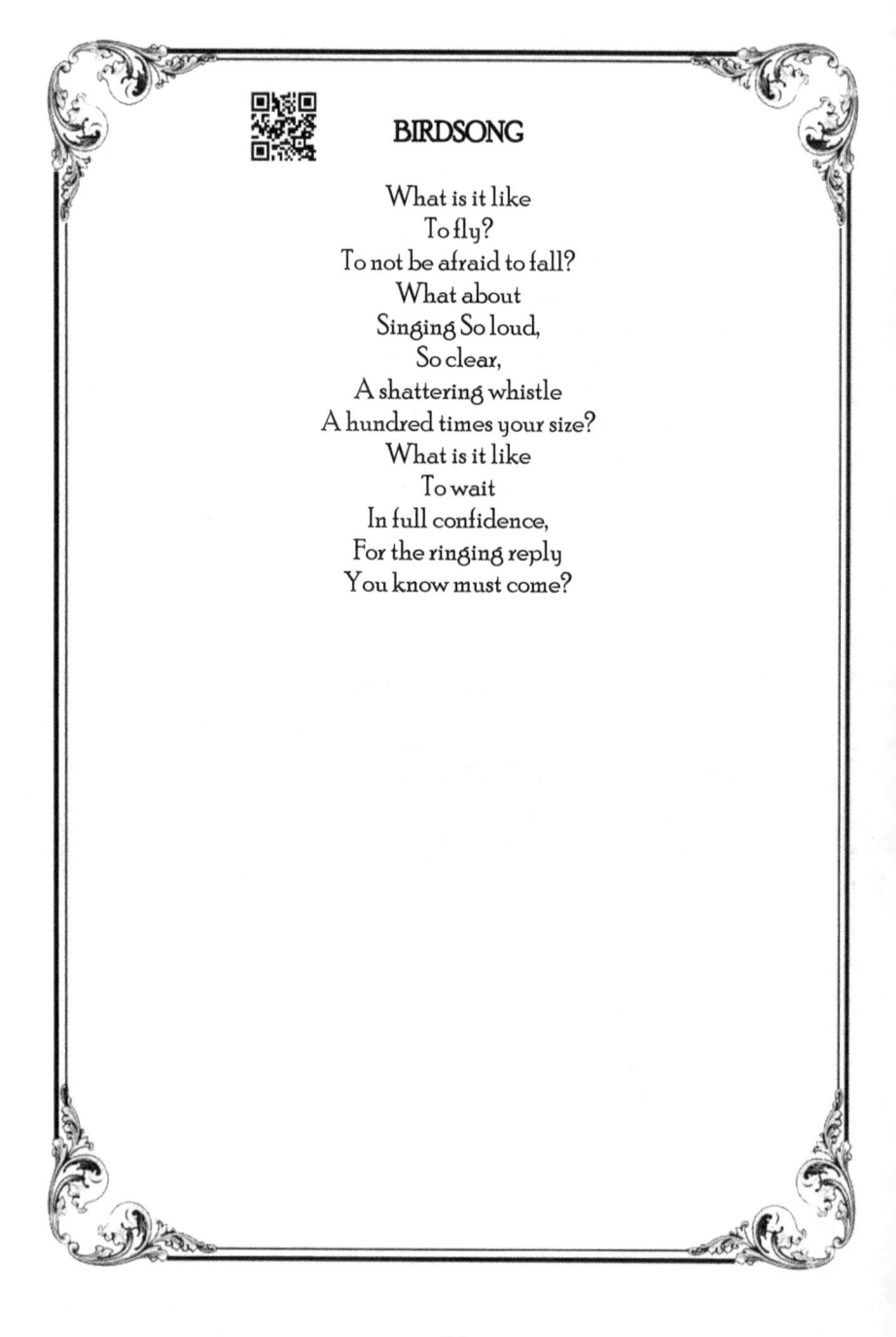

What is it like
To fly?
To not be afraid to fall?
What about
Singing So loud,
So clear,
A shattering whistle
A hundred times your size?
What is it like
To wait
In full confidence,
For the ringing reply
You know must come?

BENCH 18, MAY 31, 2017

Today is a poetry morning.

When my feet grew to size 7 1/2,
I put on my mother's
Deerskin moccasins.
In those thin-skinned shoes
Beaded by a Mohican squaw,
I walked softly in the forest and
Fallow fields with tales of Hawkeye
And Chingachgook in my head. I
Trod noiselessly, with deer and
Pheasant.

Today I pad along in my five-finger
Shoes and feel the earth just like that.
This poetry morning on the wood-chipped
Path along the shore of the
Railroad lake
Could go anywhere
 Anytime
Any place
Any century,
For I am not bound to today,
Today.

CINEMATIC DREAM

In the amber light of dawn
She died.
I was to be in the wedding
And I cried,
Folding the peach-colored bridesmaid's dress.
Carefully straightening the net ruffles;
Thinking the family would still
Go through the motions of the wedding,
Though only with the spectre of the bride.

I watched myself clearing the table
Even though I was a guest,
One who didn't know them well.
I saw the butter sitting in its boat
But couldn't think how to save it from melting.
I had to leave it there on the enormous table
Draped in white linen.

I left without saying good-byes.

Thinking;
Throughout my drive alone in the dark;
Following the narrow pavement
Between the inky folds of hills~
Unseen, but known by the contours of the road;
The only vision ~~ this blue-silver ribbon
Mounting clear to the top of each rise,
Then gone until the car

Topped the crest
To reveal the next loop
Unraveling like a skein of silky merino wool,
But only one loop at a time.
Instead of sadness at the demise of the bride
I was left with emptiness
And a taste of mercury in my mouth
That the family was carrying on with the event
Except for the feast.
The dregs of a dinner no more than a wilted salad
And a greasy butter stain on the cloth.

(It has been a year since Jamal Khasshoggi was murdered and dismembered in the Saudi consulate in Istanbul. I am still crying over it. First for the horror that the world has done nothing to call the murderers to account. I am so appalled. Second, if a journalist can be so brutally and publicly "disappeared" for speaking truth to power, how long will it be before speech is completely curtailed and our lives are no longer our own?)

CLOTHED

Her jacket is a beautiful blend
Of sky and mountain-craig colors of
Cotton.
The pattern, weavers know, is Swedish
Rosepath
Her scarf, the colors of a stormy sea.
Her trousers, pin-striped, gray on black.
Her boots are the softest leather
With a fashionable heel.
Silver rings glint attractively on
Fingers whose nails are well-manicured.
But short—not polished.
Her hair waves gently around her face,
Shiny and healthy...well-kept.

But her sweater
Is the color of blood
With black shadow shapes
Crawling directionless over the surface.

And her eyes
Are filled
With terror.

COUNTRY MOUSE – CITY HOUSE

A children's story,
"Country mouse",
Cuddles my memory.
A rock-lined path
Cavorts between
Bushes and daffodils.
Quaint afternoon teas
With miniature china
Perched on lace antimacassars.
Great Aunt So...
Lent them...
Though,
She didn't know.

Outside, leaves flutter
And lilac twigs
Squeal against the
Window glass.

Sparrows, cardinals,
House wrens and crows,
Even pheasants
Once were so familiar that
Back then, they
Were unremarkable.

THE FOREST FOR THE TREES

Sky so blue
It'd scorch your eyes
To look right at it,
Until twilight came
And changed the color
To velvet green
Just when the
Lightning bugs rose –

Rose from the grass
And robins chuckled
Their night song.

Finding comfort in familiar
Sights, smells, sounds;
They give shelter
As this
Country mouse
Settles into a city house
Amidst dangers
Jagged, raw,
Unforgiving,
Restless and unexpected;

Disconnected
Shapeless sounds,
Relentless, nagging,
Unapproachable,
Destructive
Passersby.

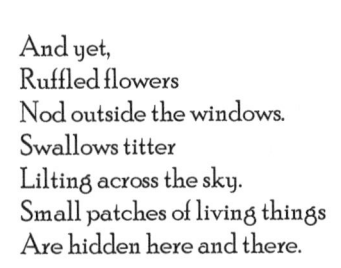

And yet,
Ruffled flowers
Nod outside the windows.
Swallows titter
Lilting across the sky.
Small patches of living things
Are hidden here and there.

Country mouse
In city house
Will be just fine
For now.

FOREST MUSIC

I went to the forest to think.
Not to hear me, with my forever rethunk thoughts;
Not what I read or heard or saw or shared.
I just longed – to hear life...
Un-interrupted.

The words I like rise from a rhythm,
And a music in my head between my ears;
But also, rising from breath, beneath my very feet.
And the best of them are still cool; dusted with earth.

I feel thoughts expand before they take shape as words.
I don't think they belong to this century,
But instead to a space of time
Before the first Great War
When my father was a boy;
Before Twentieth Century Fox.

I cannot see when I look into the light.
I only see what is reflected;
When it is past;
When it is filtered
By substance or memory.

So, here in the shade of trees,
In the shelter of the forest,
I listen for that age-older melody;
The song of nature with its words
Formed of ... natural living canons
Given to me before they wilt and wither
In contemporary musings,
Or the dry heat of habit.

HISTORY OF FEAR

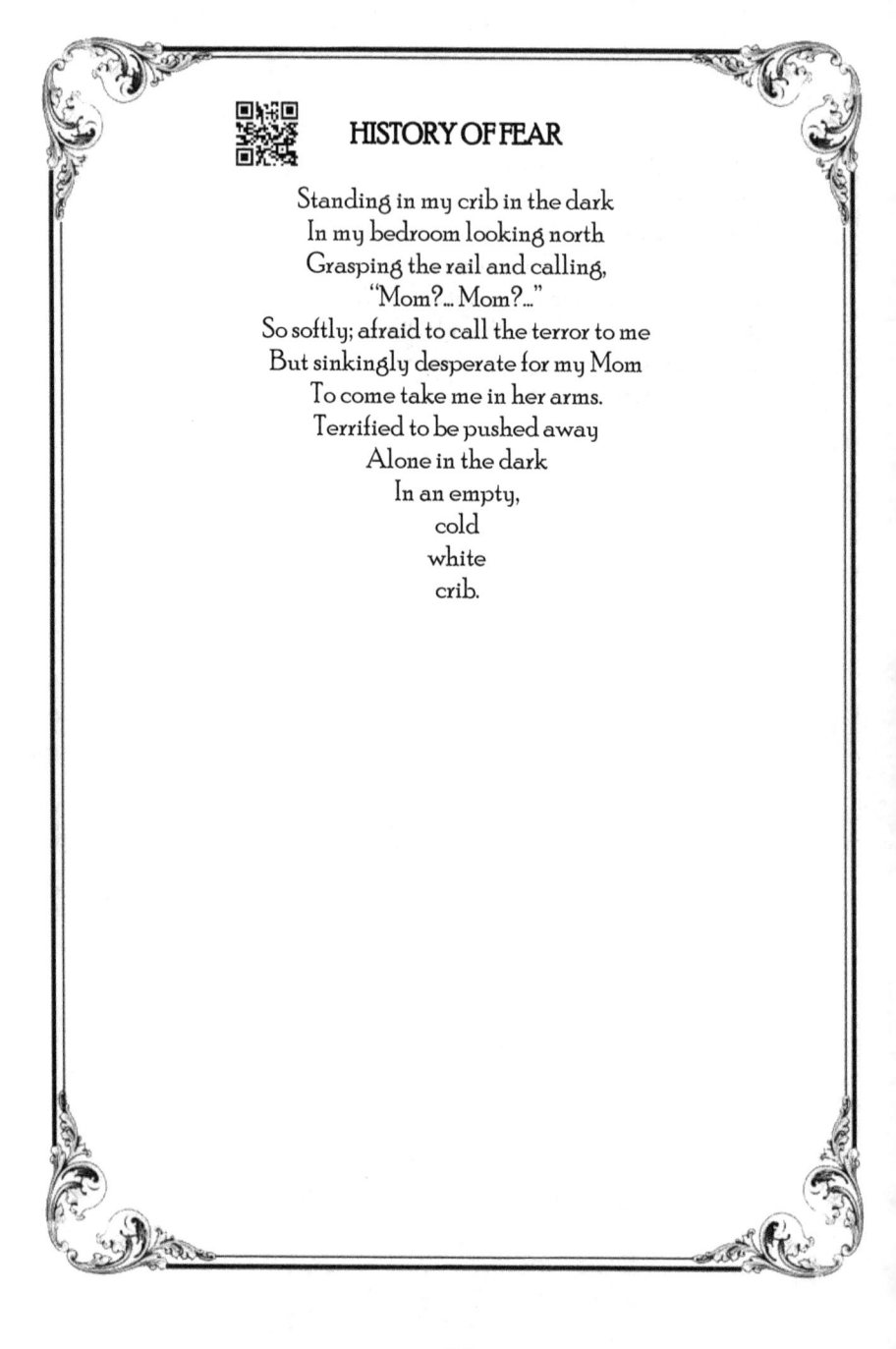

Standing in my crib in the dark
In my bedroom looking north
Grasping the rail and calling,
"Mom?... Mom?..."
So softly; afraid to call the terror to me
But sinkingly desperate for my Mom
To come take me in her arms.
Terrified to be pushed away
Alone in the dark
In an empty,
cold
white
crib.

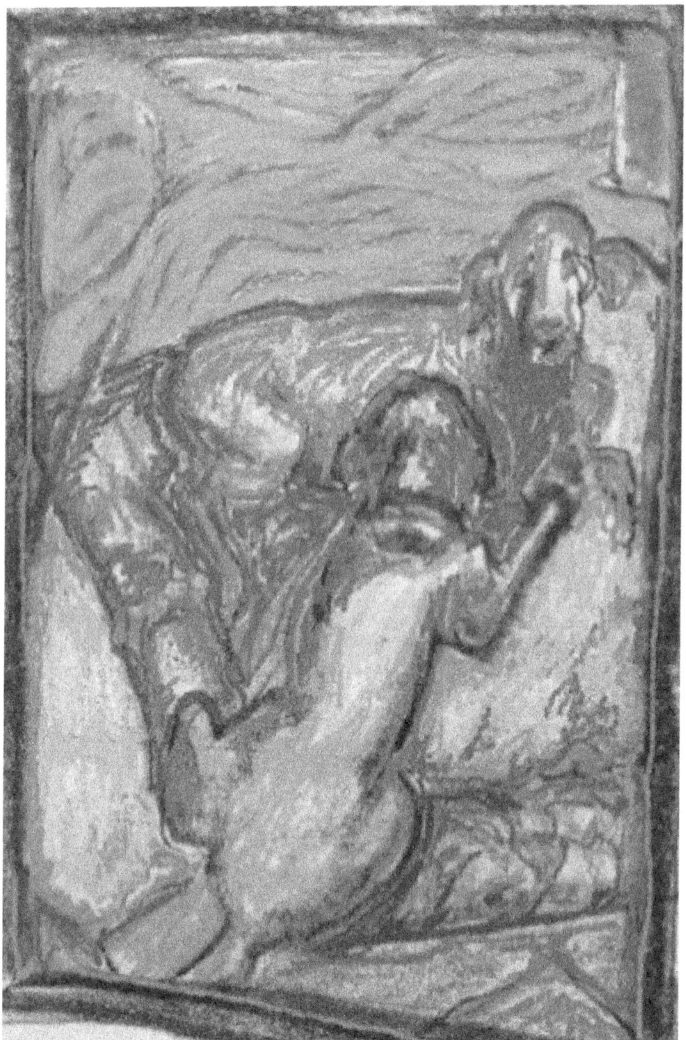

FAITH IN DOGS

I have faith in dogs;
In the "Golden-Mean",
And Three-quarter time.

Dogs know the power of a greeting.
No matter who or what you are they
Are prepared to welcome you with joy.
Dogs appreciate the meaning of
Body language.
They have a code that clearly says long
Before they come within smelling
Range if the creature before them
Means to be friendly... or not.

Looking sideways several times,
And a licking of lips says," I want to say Hello. I mean you no harm."
A steady stare means, "Beware of me.
I am stronger and meaner than you
And I am in no mood."

The thing about dogs is,
You can count on them.
They mean what they say.
And, they believe
What they see, smell and hear.
They will believe you.

The gestures they use, most times,
Are plain to see. The beauty is that if you
Are a mammal, you are programmed
To understand. Only people have pretty much
Forgotten. Sometimes they may understand
But probably don't know why.
Some deep quiet voice
Behind their ears
Can still make out that language
If only a person could be

Quiet long enough
To hear.

In the city where
We are lost in our
Accomplishments,
A dog will
Cross the sidewalk
To say a kind hello.

How much good this small gesture can do.
And how often we humans
Can subvert that simple good.

So it seems the best we all
Can do is to be like a good dog.
Be ready with a joyous greeting.
Pay attention to those around you,
So you know if they are friendly or not.

THE FOREST FOR THE TREES

Go out of your way to share your good feelings.
Stand your ground and don't run if the other
Dog looks mean. He may bite you if you do.
If you face him, you, perhaps, may change his mind.
Just this can make the world a better place.

Then... there is
Three-quarter time.
The beauty, I think, of three-quarter time
Is the lift in the middle;
The time in between the music
For me to hear myself;
In between the downbeats for a

Leap in the air, a twirl...
I delay my exhalation and
Feel a moment
Out of time, out of care
Floating for that moment

Happy and delighted,
Renewed before coming
Back to earth.

The Golden Mean speaks of
A mathematical truth.
The balance of nature which we
See, hear, and feel,
Even though we may not
Understand why.

There are the measured, metered distances
That govern light, structure, and sound.
The form of a nautilus, and
The pillars of the Parthenon.

As much as we do not often talk "dog",
As often as we ignore the lift in 3/4 time,
As often as the proof stares us
Directly in the face,
We don't believe it always
Even though...

It is the truth.

FARMER'S MARKET DAY

Sunday morning in the sun,
First cool Sunday of the fall;
Glorious bless-ed cool air to breathe;
Pools of liquid sunlight
Between shadow shoals;
Comforting...warm.

Farmers' market day;
Closer and closer
To the stands and tents
Families converge
More young than old;
Flights of laughter and smiles,
Hugs and knowing glances;

Small dogs,
Mutts and kids
And the hulking Borzoi-
Poor thing,
Bred to run,
Courser for kings,
Whose native gait rivals the wind;
Here you tread; your pace unnatural,
Slogging with your expensive human
On short thick leather leash.
Dull-eyed,
Withdrawn from the crush,
Feeling nothing,

Greeting no one ~
One step, two steps ~~
You four-footed creature
Walking in two/four time
Like your fashion forward master.

In the midst of the market scene
Our eyes meet, connect;
Go deep.
I know you. You know me.

We never knew the other's name or face,
But see what lives behind our eyes.
In one moment, a fraction of time,
With less than the speed of light,
We each recognize a kindred spirit.
It's a moment of beauty
Unmarred by conventions of speech.
A perfect moment, seen and felt,
Then gone, never to return.
Immediately submerged in the
Bright flags of conversations~
Laughter and greetings;
The promenade of see and be seen.

The walk in the park
Amidst the neighborhood crowd
Out on a Sunday morning stroll
Seems as though the air were filled
With kaleidoscope colors;
Voices colliding like brilliant butterflies
Fluttering and dancing in the pools of warm sunlight.

THE FOREST FOR THE TREES

Standing in line to buy fresh hot donuts,
The moment rises for me again.
How incredible to meet another...
To embrace without words or touch-
Another mind so completely;
Its impact felt before words could diminish the
Intimate beauty of that moment's thrill;
As satisfying as the smell of hot donuts and sugar;

As eloquent as a poem written just for us.

The moment joined to the pleasure of the day
Like a poem floating in the sunlit air,
Best because it found a suitable host;
An ear to hear, a heart to beat in time,
A mind to embrace and expand the thread of a thought.
For poetry is something like donuts.

You can't enjoy the sweetness
Till you place it on your tongue.
And once you do,
You want it again.

INDIA

I'm sorry to say~
To realize that
What defines happiness for me
Could be as trivial
As a good shower spray
A cup of black coffee
A spotless bathroom,
And a map.

FIRE

Didja ever blow on a match
To put out a flame?
It works, and all that remains
Of the fire is a glowing ember.
When you hold the flint
Under a dribble of water
From the kitchen gooseneck faucet,
All you hear is a short hiss
And it is gone; cold enough
To discard in the trash.
Cold enough that it may not
Have burned at all.

Didja ever burn leaves in the backyard?
We would rake our White Oak's
Blunt-fingered leaves
Into long berms
On the winding gravel drive
And set them alight.

When coals had formed like
The glowing flints of a thousand matches,
We would throw acorns in
To hear them explode like
The report of a rifle.

But, ...blow on that flame
And it could suddenly
Leap out of control.
Hot tongues of flame
And little live coals from
Exploding acorns
Easily escape to the leaf cover
Not yet raked.

One fall day a sudden west wind
Swooped in and turned
Our long, carefully-shaped shock of leaves
Into a roaring blaze
Which caught not just
The nearby leaves,
But also the family car,
And in no time caused
The gas can sitting there
To explode...

Nothing like little pops of bursting acorns,
But more like our whole world
Had suddenly turned to gas, heat and flame.

The fire truck, summoned, was on the way,
But not arrived before the flaming car parts
Had ignited the cedar shakes on the house roof.

That is when I remembered the ironic look
Of burned out houses. You've seen them before.
The only thing still standing? – Their chimneys.

Fortunately, the pumper truck roared up the drive
By then and pumped gallons of water
Over the roof, the car, and our neat snake
Of blackened leaves.

Soon the fire was out,
And the next day,
After hours of hissing,
Smoking, cracking and sighing,
The fire was out; cold enough to touch;
To walk through, but never cold enough to
Erase what was left of our confidence in fire.

FOREST STORY

Seek spirit by the shores of the lake.
Look for wildness in the shadows there.
I take my wild spirit to rejoice in the lake.
Where the cat tails whisper to the tree frogs.

Beneath the rippled surface, deep currents run,
Spears of light reflect on the surfaces of leaves,
But they don't stop there.
The rays don't rest there.
They penetrate,
Driving processes we know of,
But don't see with our everyday eyes.

Oh, it is difficult work today to be wild.
Even to be here with wild things.
Their tremulous voices rise
But are so easily drowned by the sound
Of jets and train whistles; the distant growl of traffic;
Relentless footfalls of human endeavor that all but obliterate the forest's song.
This forest, though protected by people is badly abused by them.
It is only allowed within acceptable boundaries.

THE FOREST FOR THE TREES

Breezes still play here, skipping over lake ripples, wafting over maple leaves,
Caressing the feathers of the smallest wren, grandfather Heron, and the baby owl.
Watery reflections anchor the struggling trees.
Wavelets lap the miniature islands of grass,
Whose seeds mistakenly sprouted on a broken log lodged in the muddy shore.

Even as the civilized cacophony ebbs and flows,
The breeze here, strengthens, waking the taller trees
To weigh in as the lake waves splash.
Fishes arc into the air for a buggy morsel; birds vie for territory,
And the human footfalls fade in the distance.

Ah, this is what I came here for:
A moment of wildness;
This fabric I belong to without ambition or judgment or greed.
I hear an ancient song that fades as people ignore it.
I come here with my wild spirit
To hear the echo of wildness I belong to,
...we belong to,
And eschew at our peril.

GLANCE AT BONNIE'S JAZZ SCORE / A TALE OF TWO SCORES

Five lines; four spaces,
A picture of time and tone,
Filled with music;
Beauty in sculpted harmony;

Each moment punctuated
Like an essay –
The tempo decided,
Described in Italian
So that each measure, each phrase,
Each breath is clear.
The meaning clear
With no question or argument;
Performed the same
Identical way for centuries;

The composer's intent
Reaching through the years
So we know him
As though he lived next door,
And we just shared tea and crumpets.
So satisfying...
I could listen all day.

THE FOREST FOR THE TREES

But then,
Along comes this new guy.
He says,
"Tea is just weak coffee.
Crumpets are muffins and butter.
...I need a new song –
Something fresher than a hundred years old."

Like Jack Benny smirked in Delmonico's
When the waiter proudly announced,
"Sir, we serve the same cheesecake we made for Diamond Jim Brady
In the year eighteen hundred and ninety."
Benny then quipped, in his special 'Jack' way,
"Can't you bring me something fresher today?"

So, with that same old melody behind him,
The new guy freely played what was in his bones.
And, his ir-reverence didn't fit
In five lines and four spaces.
It flew all over the page!
And OFF the page...

And caught the ear of a sax player
Who looked over his shoulder at the melody,
And it struck him in the heart
And he played another tune
That merged and tickled and delighted a drummer
Who made those two songs together, ROCK!

And when a singer heard it,
Her ears swooned,
And she sang her song along too.

All that jazz, it sounded just great,
And got feet to tapping;
Folks to swaying and smiling.

The next day
That ir-reverent man
Played his melody again,
And the melody came out the same,
...only different.

As each player added her ears,
His heart, their dis-satisfaction,
The page still only carried that one line of melody.
The jazz players did the rest.
All because that irreverence had to smile or cry
And just couldn't fit on the page.

It needed more than five lines;
   ... four spaces.

MISTRAS

Hurry! Write it down before it fades!
The sounds of the church bell
Move the air in the valley.
A cacophonous chorus of distant dogs
Bounces off the warm stone wall.
(Somebody should feed them)
And,
Was it the sound of the air?
Blue misted, defying science,
The impossible air that glows as
The day's light recedes,
And the sky expands to envelope the hills.

Here in this valley where the Spartans
Reportedly threw babes from the cliffs,
In a way, night does not fall here;
The hills also rise up into the darkening sky,
So, you should know, the babes were saved
And raised in secret by shepherds.

How can I forget?
Words of the song we sang together
Driving up the switch backs
Singing with laughter
While we waited for the nanny goat
With her swinging udders and
Fast following, wild-eyed kid.

HALFDARK

Down the stairs in the half dark-
Six o'clock in the morning –
My summer bag crouches
In the corner of the hallway
By the leaded glass door.
It may not be what it seems.

My summer bag crouches in the corner
Like the Cheshire cat.
If I go back up the stairs
And come back down again,
I wonder if it will grin?
Grin that wide-mouth, head-wide smile?

For though it is just a crocheted string bag
I thoughtlessly fill with miscellany
And throw it here and throw it there:
Over my shoulder, into the car,
On the floor of the hall;
Some artisan reached deep inside
To plan the pattern,
Choose the colors so pleasing to me,
And then proceeded
Stitch by stitch,
To bring this bag to life –
Designed with a purpose in mind.

Down the stairs, half-dark
In the morning, six o'clock -
My summer bag crouches
In the corner
By the couch.

Oh!... forgot something;
Back I go up the stairs,
And on the descent,
Did it grin?
Will it pounce?
What persistent, grinning,
Cheshire cat
Life did the artisan
Stitch inside?

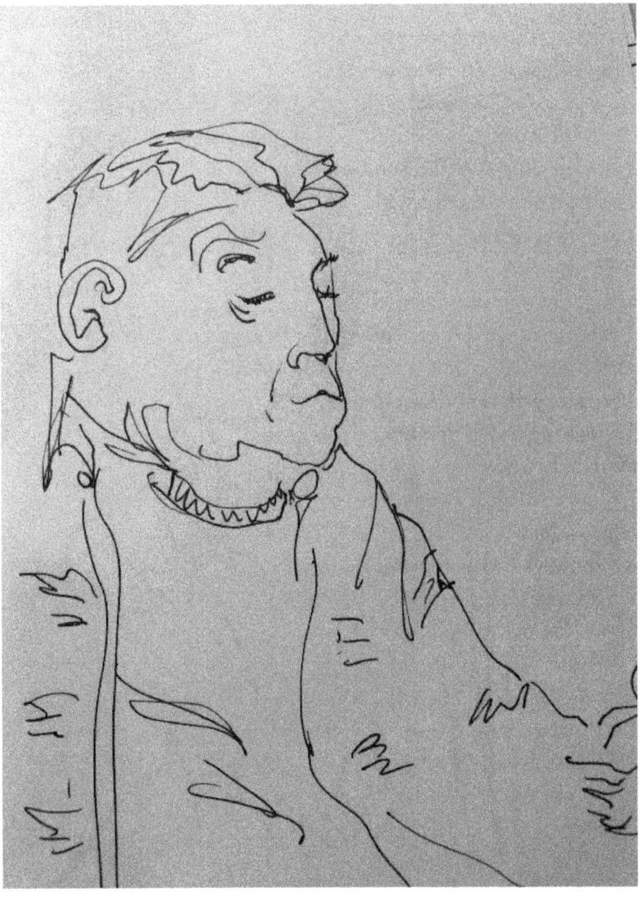

HORACE

Turns out, Horace likes leashes.
The feel of a thick leather loop
Surrounding his hand,
And the better sensation
Of wrapping the leather length
Round and round his wrist.
No telling why,
But there it is.

Somehow, you'd think the longer the better,
But for Horace, that would allow the dog
Too much distance for comfort.
Better to have him cinched up close.
No doubt about who's who
When the leash is less than seven feet long.

Then there is the question
Of what kind of leather,
How thick, and how wide,
Natural, oiled, or dyed.
He much prefers his loop
Natural and oiled and
Better to be not thinner than
An eighth of an inch.
There is less chance of breakage.

Horace apparently spends a lot of time
Considering the requirements of leashes.
It is quite a satisfying pastime,
But he will not consider
Getting a dog.

INSIDE MY HEART
or
NIGHT ON THE FARM

Each night I walk the same path.
Gravel crunches at each step.
Hedge glides by on my right.
Stars abide thinly, far away.

Each night I walk from house to barn.
Each night I walk back from barn to house.
No strangers cross my path.
No cars or buses bar my way.
Nothing changes to remark on.
And yet,
Each night along the way,
Something catches my eye.
Something new delights me.
In all the sameness, nuance lives.

Each night I see in a different way,
A star or cloud white against dark sky,
A tree silhouetted against the ridge,
A glancing shaft of light passes through a bush.
Starlight gleam shines from the surface of the pond.
Here it is,
The internal surface of my heart –
Open for me to see.

OF AN AGE
(PRIVATE JOKE FROM A TREEFUL OF PIGS)

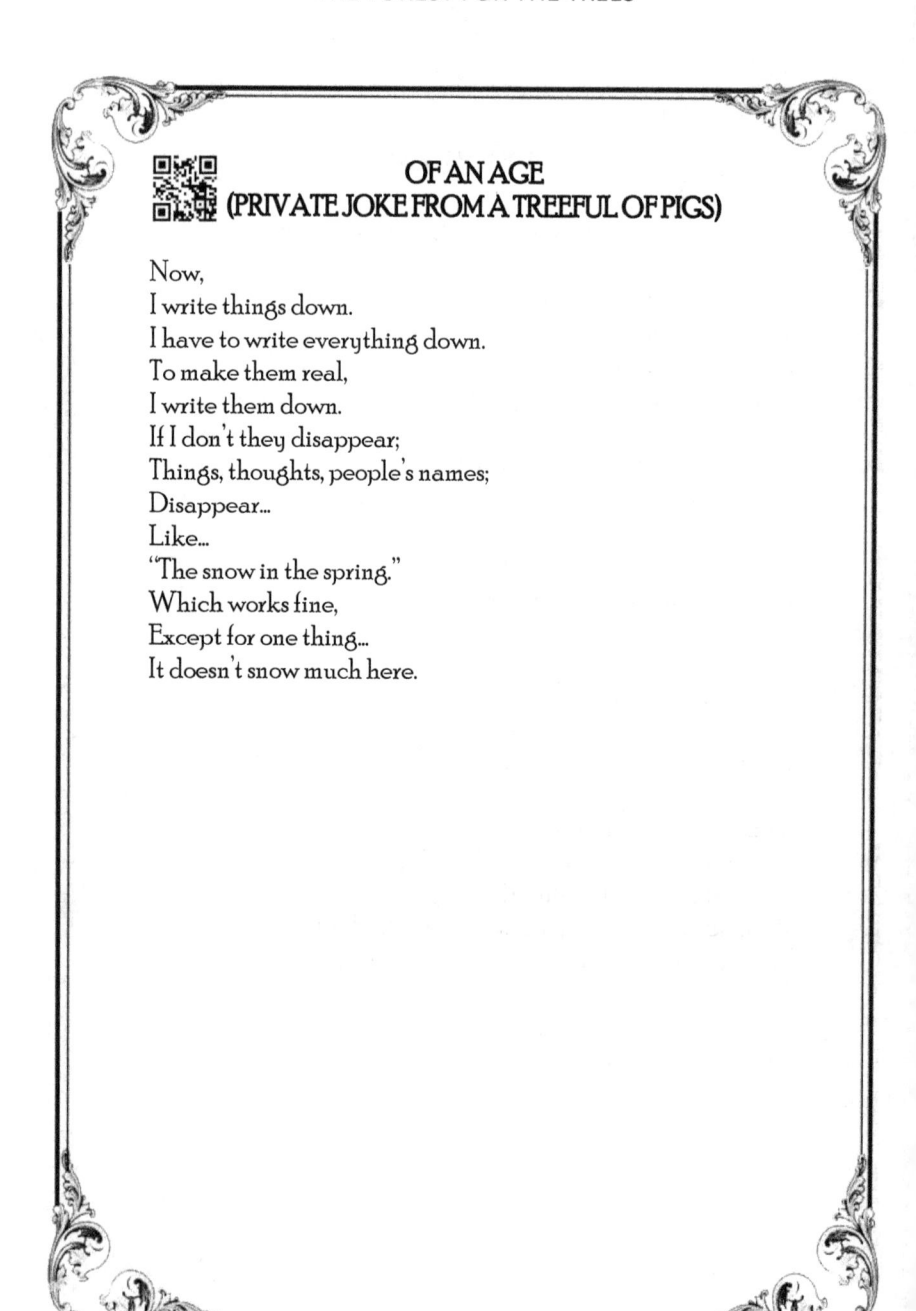

Now,
I write things down.
I have to write everything down.
To make them real,
I write them down.
If I don't they disappear;
Things, thoughts, people's names;
Disappear...
Like...
"The snow in the spring."
Which works fine,
Except for one thing...
It doesn't snow much here.

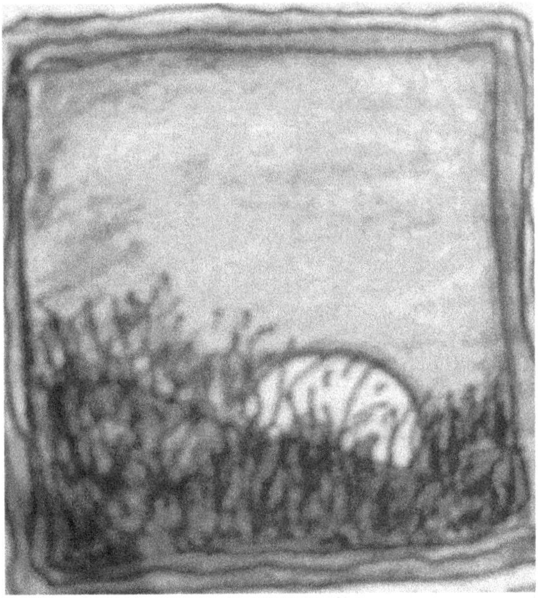

LIMITLESS

We each contain an inner child.
How do we know her?
She is the center of her universe.
She hears the truth hidden
Behind "acceptable" words.
She believes she is the only one
Who can hear it.
The only one to embrace it,
And, she believes,
She will, probably, regret it.

Wouldn't it be nice to tell her,
It's ok.
You are not alone.
We hear it too.
We also hold it in our hearts.
And, just at that moment,
We may stop and agree,
We will probably get hurt
Because of it.
And, deep inside, we are each
The center of our own universe.
Though we agree it may not literally be true.

Today my child peeked out peculiarly
Because I walked barefoot
On the rainy city sidewalk.
Back and forth from my front door
To my daughter's car
In a raincoat, PJs and
NO SHOES.

What a renegade!
How daring!
How suddenly connected through the

Whole of my life's history to the
Time when, at four years old,
I ran barefoot

On icy cold summer grass
So cold I could hardly stand it,
Alone since my parents were still asleep in their bed
And I dared unlock the door
To run outside
Barefoot
Alone in my own universe.

Just as today when I tiptoed on
The delicious, wet concrete and met no one,
All those years ago, no one knew I
Was such a daring success, such a
Wild, limitless thing!
And today I felt the same;
DARING! LIMITLESS! DELIGHTED!
Just from feeling my feet
Running barefoot on the street.

NOSES

I love her nose;
Narrow between the eyes
With a lilt at the end.
It describes her character –
Certainly not narrow-minded,
But serious, passionate, and caring
With a lilt of humor and caprice
When times call for it.

Darling girl,
Living embodiment of love;
Complete with all the complications
Belonging to us all.

I am becoming familiar with his nose;
Also narrow between the eyes,
But then straight and muscled;
Consistent all the way to the end –
No lilt at the tip
But instead, straight and clear.

That straight run to the precipice
Could be the tragedy for him.
Once the course is decided,
His character must cleave him to the path.
There is no lilt at the tipping point
To steer him back from his ultimate fate.

MEGARO MOUSIKIS
(Greek for GREAT HALL OF MUSIC)

Our room in the hotel
Was two eleven
With a view of the sea.
Across the hall and down a pace
In room two hundred three,
We could hear 'Eroica' – just a phrase,
A violin's haunting voice practicing the theme.
Later, we heard snippets of Mendelssohn's
'The Hebrides', and a little from Debussy.
Other difficult passages
Were worried; chewed on,
Like a predator dismembering its prey –
Each time – voiced with more precision.
Sometimes, only one note we would hear
But that note after a while, in its solitude,
Would sing!

For four days he played.
No matter what time of day or night,
We would go by and drink
The measures as they escaped his door.
Hour after hour the music went on.

~ ~ ~

On Tuesday night, at the Mégaro Mousikís,
We got finally to see
Who our mystery musician might be;

THE FOREST FOR THE TREES

The soloist, a young man, with dark, chin-length hair,
Slim of build, standing humbly before us on the stage.
He and the orchestra sent their notes singing toward the sky.
And the great hall lived up to its name.
The music filled us up
And overflowed the space
Making one being of all the audience.

We cheered and clapped and thumped the floor,
And the musicians answered with more fervor than before.
And at the height of our frenzy, ... suddenly,

The lights went out...
The musicians, gamely, played on for a measure or more,
But that was all.

Slowly, after the announcement came that the lights could not be restored,
We could hear the musicians scraping their chairs, hefting their instruments,
And amid a buzz of conversation we all began to leave.
Slowly, raggedly, feeling our way in the dark,
We wound our way away from the Mégaro Mousikís,
And followed the dim edge of the quay back to our hotel.

No sound came now from two hundred and three.
Our humble genius was gone.
The deserted hall felt haunted, deprived of the strains
Of the slender, humble young man, with dark chin-length hair
Who played at the Mégaro Mousikís.

MONDAY EVENING 1

My favorite place is just above the treetops
Where the clouds stretch beyond the horizon;
Where the distinction between fancy and reality
Means less than nothing in the thin air.

A picture of surf pounding the sand,
So real you can hear its thunder
Vanishes in a moment with a change of the wind
Less than nothing in the thin air.

It's here I find a magic domain;
The cloudscape where my thoughts
Can soar and dip
In the lands beyond the wind,
Less than nothing in the thin air.

In the lands beyond the wind
Where I am not bound by should,
Or could, or would,
Not burdened by "not done";
Promises not kept,

In the lands beyond the wind
All those dear and bumptious cares
Shift with the breeze
From chains and weights
To perfumed breath;
Pure;
Surreal;
Less than nothing in the thin air.

ODE TO THESSALONIKI

Mythical walk
By the mythical sea,
The mythical mountains
Flanking the lea,
Who should be walking,
But mythical me?

The sea is dark – bluer;
The sky far too light.
The mountains much farther;
The ships?
Close, too bright.

Joggers racing
Down and up the wharf
Pass Alexander
Astride Bucephalus,
But none of them look.

The general strikes me with awe,
And moreso his horse.
But then, they are only stone
Not live with me.
Still I can imagine

On my mythical walk,
By the mythical sea,
The mythical mountains
Flanking the lea,
Who should be walking
But mythical me?

OH MY STAR

Oh my star
You burn so bright
Brighter than eyes can bear to see
I pray this glittering path –
Your flight,
Won't be cut short tonight.

RADNOR LAKE OCTOBER 26

The best place to practice the Tai Chi form
Is on the platform by the lake.
Looking north, I school myself
To enjoy the life and place
Where I live now.
Lucky, lucky me.

But then, I saw persimmons on the path,
One squashed, one not,
And I am back
15 years past
Watching our little pony
Razi, eat his fill
Ending up drunk and full,
Suffering a terrible tummy ache.
Oh,...
How he loved persimmons.
Of all the horses,
He was the only one
Who ate them, too.

And, he is gone.
Tears sting my eyes.
My breath stops,
Catching way before my throat,
Thickened, stymied,
Felled by grief.

POEM ~~ TREE

Didja ever hug a tree?
Huh...
Not me.
Except when I was three.
And then, 'cause
We were playing
Hide and seek.
I hugged an oak
So it would
Hide me.
Well...
I do remember
At thirteen,
Leaning
My tear-hot face
On my hands
On the same rough bark
Of the tree,
The self-same oak
Who hid me
At three.
Oh, and there was a time,
How old was I?
Took a book to that tree
When the day was long and
No one needed me;
Sitting down at the root
Found a place
Between its knees.
Oh, ancient tree,
That time, it hugged me.

THE FOREST FOR THE TREES

Bark warm, comforting
Between my shoulder blades
Yet cutting hard against my back;
Spine to spine,

Its roots deep, searching
The vitals of our earth;
Its solid, living bark –

Skin soft in the core
With fibers running unsullied
From root to crown
Delivering water,
Its life's blood,
To tender leaves
Open to the sky and sun.
Not a thing that's extra
Nor unneedful; every structure
Informed by gravity;
Its form dictated by
Natural forces
To grow in fullness
To its ever increasing height;
Tons of heavy structural wood,
Seemingly immovable
And therefore dead like stone.
But there is the error,
Human indeed, to assume,
For instead, that tree
Must be a sentient being.
It grows.
It heals its wounds,
And changes with the seasons.

And proof of all proof,
It nurtured me;
Was Father, Mother, Confidant and Friend,
And with its stern bulk,
A pastor teaching by example
For the life of me.
So, I guess I am wrong.
For though I thought not,
I did hug a tree.

RETURN FROM QUITO

Today we descended from the sky,
Returned from a foreign land
Where the inhabitants SING their language.
High, high with their ears in the heavens,
Brushing shoulders with the clouds;
Drinking rain in the afternoons
When those clouds sweep down swallowing the streets;

Back from the land that time forgot,
To time as commodity, lord and tyrant;
To home familiar and yet foreign;
Here where I am stranger than in
Those strange lands,
Where though foreign, I was seen as friend.

Here I am more akin to the city
Trees standing in silent witness
To the foreign people
Passing each other by,
With ears and eyes stopped
By their preoccupations;
Having missed the chance
To be here in their own land;
Missed the moment
To see me friend.

What are we afraid of?
Are we simply out of practice?
Or are we held socially enthralled
In a fairy tale of our own making?
I hope we don't have to sleep
For one hundred years
To escape the spell.

WHAT TO DO WITH GRIEF

Tears sting my eyes.
My breath stops,
Catching way before my throat,
Thickened, stymied,
Felled by grief.

My question is, how do we carry
On with this?
How do we lift this load and not
Visit it on others?
The ones we love, the young ones
Who know nothing of this
But only suspect;

Our companions, who know but
Have their own burdens;
Do we drink this together and
Suffer the hangover,
Wallowing in the stench of
Regurgitated pain?

Or, do we jam it back in our
Pockets ~~~
Close to the chest
And build our own iron lung to
Breathe more life into an old loss?

Is there a way to transform grief?
Make use of it for good?
I have seen beauty in a few old faces.
My guess is, this is what they have done.
I still don't know how they do it,
But at least it can be done.

REALLY?

Often people say that trees are standing still.
But, really?
They are all busily growing up.
It is we distracted humans who rush
Around on the ground and forget
To grow up.

SOUP

Beethoven may have said it best.
"A man who lies can not make good soup."
Ludwig, what are you talking about?
Did your Ninth waft out of a soup pot?
Ridiculous,...and yet,...

A good soup is a pleasure,
Better with fresh onion and garlic,
Sautéed in rich butter and oil.
The stock, a living liquid;
Bones and whole stalks of celery,
Crackling sweet carrots,
Foot high leaves of tender Dandelion,
A little lemon – with zest,
A bay leaf that grew happy by the salt sea
Spiced with pepper from Madagascar
Where the tropical birds perch in their splendour
Just resting from their tour of the sky.

And each of these vegetables,
Fruits of the vast earth,
Are nothing without
Fresh, pure rain
And sweet warm sunlight
And time, thyme by the handful,
You can't define with a cup measure.
All these ingredients must be added with
Their full complement of time.

Pretense only spoils the taste,
For if a necessary ingredient is
Missing, or spoiled, or harvested before it has grown
To full ripeness,
No one will want to eat it.
Without hesitation, they will know,
It is NOT.GOOD. SOUP.

So, a man without patience or heart
To wait for the right ingredients to give up their best;
Who calls his stew what it is not,
No matter how hard he wills it
Will be exposed in the end
By his pot of dross.
As Beethoven put it so well,
"A man who lies can not make good soup." –– or music.

SPOKEN: UNSPOKEN

THE STORY UNFOLDED AGAIN.
THREE DAYS IN A ROW
IT CAME UNBIDDEN.
HE HEARD THE WORDS
AS THEY LEFT HIS MOUTH.

HE STOPPED JUST SHORT
OF THE WORST OF HIS PAIN
WHERE HE BORE WITNESS
TO THE UNSPEAKABLE.

YOU MIGHT ASK, 'WHY'?
WHY SAY IT AGAIN?
WHY LOOK AT THAT
WHICH WAS TEARING
FRESH TEARS FROM HIS HEART
YET AGAIN?

AND WHY NOW?
IN THE HANDSHAKE RENEWAL
OF A RELATIVE'S VISIT?

BECAUSE IN THE EMBRACE OF TRUE REGARD
SHARING THE BEST AND THE WORST,
WE HEAR THE PARAMETERS SHAPING US,
AND QUICK, BEFORE WE SEPARATE AGAIN,
SURROUND THE DRIED WITHERED FRUITS
OF REGRETS WITH LOVING HANDS AND
PUSH THEM OUT, SHOO THEM ON THEIR WAY.

THE FOREST FOR THE TREES

AT THE SAME MOMENT, WITH SILVER-CLOTHED
HANDS WE POLISH THE GEM-STONES OF
THE BEST OF OUR UTTERANCES.
SHINE WARM LIGHT ON THEM.
WATER THEM AND FEED THEM.
SMILE AT THEM, AND LOOK!

THE SAD AWFUL DEMONS HAVE SHRUNK.
WE STARVED THEM OF THEIR POWER,
AND THOUGH THEY MAY STILL LURK
AT THE LIMITS OF OUR VISION,
WE HAVE FOUND THE STONES TO BUILD A FORTRESS
OF GOOD SOLID FEELING,
AND NOURISHED THE BRIGHT SHAFTS OF LIGHT –
THE BEAMS OF WARMTH AND CLARITY
THAT SHIELD US WHEN
WE WALK OUT IN THE SHADOWS OF OUR FEARS.

SHADOW WALK

This morning, walking west,
My shadow glides before me.
Very pleasing, that shadow,
Tall and slender;
Shouldering the terrain with ease.

Sliding courage,
Shadow hair bouncing,
Flowing like quick silver;
Passing gently o'er the stones;

Walk lightly,
Like a shadow...
Guest of the earth,

For,...
If I walk this way again
This evening
My shadow will be behind me.
With the day behind me,
When it is filled with choices
Good and bad,
Will I like my shadow as well?

I hope to walk through my days
So I like my shadow
As much at the end,
As at break of day.

SNOWFLAKING

The world around Nashville
Is getting a good wash today.
All the dust and pollen
Left on the leaf-bare trees
Is running down the street
In miniature rivers;
Swollen and furious,
Though small.

Would that it would wash
The dust and grime
From human interaction
Leaving it washed and fresh and new.

The poison of bigotry,
The dust of egotism,
The grime of misjudgment and misunderstanding;
It all could use a good wash.

The torrent outside turned to snowflaking by afternoon.
Frozen jewelry melting, cooling, flake by flake,
The gritty concrete of the pavement.
Would that it would cool our human angst.

THE BLOWS OF TIME

My fingers trace this scarred and barren field
Which once was full and ripe to bursting,
Where, of a time, I tasted, running
Fingers through verdant soil;
Rejoicing as I kneeled
Open-hearted with innocent eyes.

Life has dealt its blows.
And though we rise again,
Each time it knocks us senseless,
Every fall has left its mark.
Here the raised white line
Left from the surgeon's knife;
There a pit depressed –
Its bounds, the mark of an old blow
Not quite ever healed.

Thinning, paperish skin
Slowly losing its ability
To color with emotion,
Is yet revealing
The structural bone;
The grit which resists
The blows of time.

THE DIAGNOSIS

One man's conclusion
Hangs – hovers above us
Like a noose.
We know each detail of the rope:
The bristling, stinging hairs protruding;
Rubbed patches of dry rot,
Clumps of clinging clay and trash,
Where the rope had dragged in the mud,
Then dried or moldered still wet and slimed;
Scraped in places 'til it resembles an old
Flea-bitten pelt. Putrified,
Smelling like death,
Strings of road-kill twined and strangled.
A breeze blows the noose up and away,
And we eagerly forget
Sight and sound and smell of
The Diagnosis as it hangs above us
Just out of sight.

In that moment we see each other sweetly.
Love, like a thirst coats all our words and actions...
Dagger sweet it pierces deeper than our first infatuation~
A lifetime of courting and argument, striving and forgiving.
It cuts deeper in that moment than ever before.
What wonder is this?

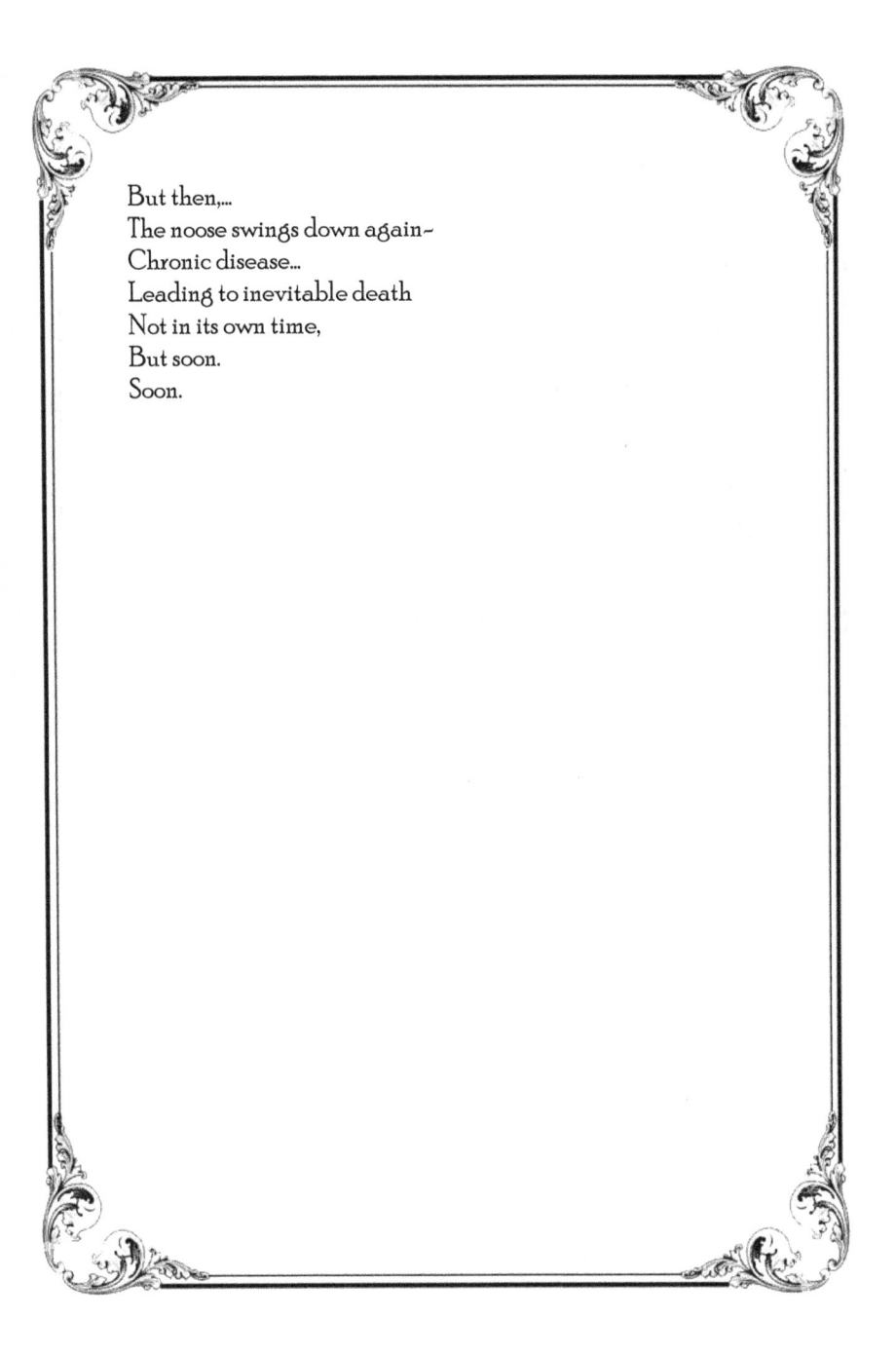

But then,...
The noose swings down again-
Chronic disease...
Leading to inevitable death
Not in its own time,
But soon.
Soon.

THE DOGS ARE GONE

"Hi, how are you?"
SILENCE.
She finally says, "The dogs are gone. Three days."
SILENCE
Everyone's nightmare: to lose those you love.
Each day a torture; not knowing:
Tuesday,...Wednesday,... Thursday,...
NOW,...
I don't want to call again.
What if it's bad news?
Finally, Friday, I have to call.
She says, "Tomorrow a friend is coming,
Bringing her search and rescue dog."
SILENCE.
My thoughts follow her...
Three days more.
Saturday,...Sunday,...Monday,...
This time I only have the courage to text:
"I hope the dogs are home."
She CALLS back, and replies, "Haven't you heard?
We found them Saturday; Buried them in the backyard
Sunday.
Can't talk about it."
SILENCE.
The nightmare, no longer a dream;
Overwhelming,
All-encompassing sadness
At the void left by Willy and Teig.

Becomes a relentless pain,
A rent in the fabric,
A blooming stain,
Making up,...
SILENCE. THE WORDS DON'T COME.
With every birth, every triumph, or so it seems,
In the balance of life,

Comes a death, a failure.
With every glittering, joyful celebration along the way,
Follows the dark, the painful day to be endured.
How do we color the story of our lives?
What do we construct of these conflicts?
What mechanisms are there that translate
Each high, each low
Into the Persona –
That becomes me, or you?
SILENCE. THE WORDS DON'T COME.

THE SONG

Your song is strong,
Loud
And sure.

Mine is quiet,
Tentative,
And soft.

Say me this:
When a raindrop falls
Into a concrete pipe,
Does it follow
Its destiny?

The fate I expected
For my lovely raindrop
Was to water the roots
Of a sapling;

To joyfully nurture that young,
Tender spire ~
A sprout meant to grow
Into a towering tree.

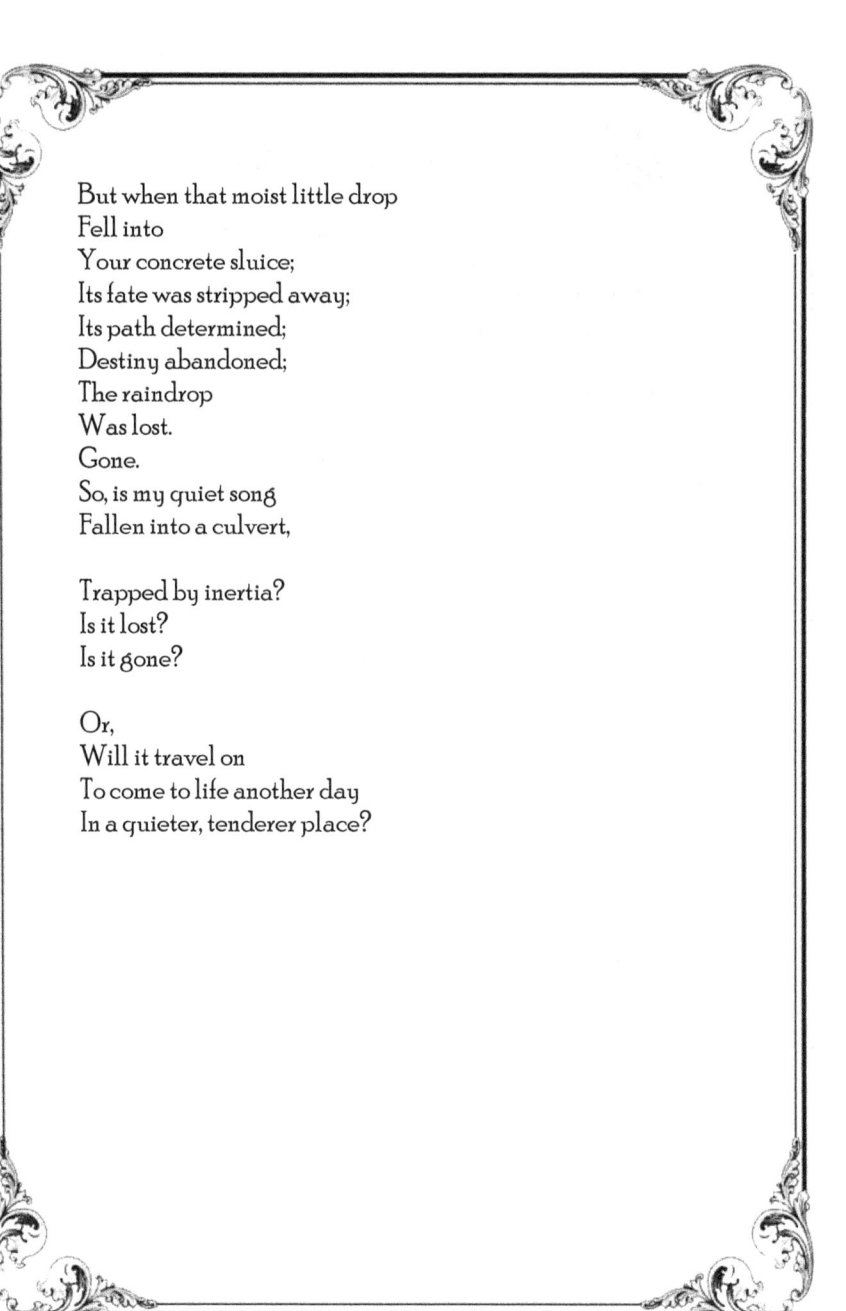

But when that moist little drop
Fell into
Your concrete sluice;
Its fate was stripped away;
Its path determined;
Destiny abandoned;
The raindrop
Was lost.
Gone.
So, is my quiet song
Fallen into a culvert,

Trapped by inertia?
Is it lost?
Is it gone?

Or,
Will it travel on
To come to life another day
In a quieter, tenderer place?

THE USES OF MELANCHOLY

Here am I in a near constant state of waking dream.
Half alive, half aware. Drifting purposeless.
Oh, when something is required, it gets done,
But the zest, the joy, is gone.

On another hand,
Isn't it this very detachment
That makes social commentary possible?
We cannot witness that in which we are fully immersed.

Sure, most of what forms into words
Coalesces into phrases that have lived
In someone else's mind before.
But, isn't that what makes those utterances universal?

Thoughts that reach backward in time
To paint a unique portrait perched somewhere along the
branch of man's evolution
Never quite erase the common theme;
The culmination of all that has gone before.

It must be this connection that allows those who live
Through sadness and loss
To weather sad events with joy radiating from their faces.

And, what about the ravages of body and mind?
The wounds that others are not invited to witness?
I see men and women who have survived great sorrow
Who look excruciatingly beautiful to me.
A depth and sweetness appears in the best of them.
We each have a choice when faced with hard times.
Either experience can curdle and sour us,
Or it can temper and hone the goodness already there.

I know two healers of note who
Realized early on, that the war veterans
They met at Angel Fire,
Whom previous therapies had failed,

Were suffering from more...
...than the Viet Nam War.
The final break was the result of many burdens, not just one,
And true healing had to address them all.

I would like to know, was it also past existences,
Or only contemporary hurts?
Were the healings curing injuries of this life
Or, some gathering of atoms randomly combined,
Remnants of exploded stars...?

These melancholy thoughts loomed large in my mind
Until they appeared on the page.
Suddenly they shrank alarmingly!
These miniature musings...

Still, profound or not, perhaps it can be of help –
To set them down here, all in one place.
Pin them down in close proximity
So they can clasp hands
And maybe, just maybe, dance;
Forming a sad quadrille –
A line of dancing words stepping to shared music–
Capable of turning sadness to gratitude;
Healing tears to a melancholy smile.

THE WILDFLOWERS ARE GOING WILD

After a short night's sleep,
I took my headache to the park
And reveled in the woods.
A downy woodpecker greeted me.
I watched a hiker wearing earbuds, staring at the ground
Almost walk over a pair of Canada Geese, resting on the path.
Geez Lou-eez! Go walk on the sidewalks.

And all this time,
The wildflowers were going wild! Spring Beauties,
Dutchman's Britches, Trout Lilies, Trillium, Blue Delphinium.
My mother's voice in my head named each blooming example.
Of course, I was small when she held forth.
The thrill was to come unexpectedly upon them; the Shooting
Stars, Solomon Seal, Hepatica, Grape Hyacinth, Jack-in-the-
Pulpit, May Apples, Dog Tooth Violets, Violets- Purple and
White, Blue-eyed grass!
Later in life, living near different forests, I learned new names
like Skunk Cabbage, Fiddlehead Ferns, Lady's Slipper and
Ranunculus.
Why is the naming of living things such a pleasure?
Wildflowers tell a familiar story,
And each year
When I call each fleeting flower by name.
I summon not only the flowering time,
But the invisible winter metamorphosis;
The tiny seed cracked by the frost
Heaved up out of its burial place,
Pillowed in the mud to
Burst out of its carapace
To grow into fingering roots;

THE FOREST FOR THE TREES

Clutching dirt and pebbles for
Sustenance and support
Strong enough to brace the
Upright stem pushing earnestly toward the light.

Strong and ruthless,
Demolishing every obstacle it can't avoid...

How does it end in such a
Delicate fairy wing of a bloom?
Such a fragile, short-lived thing?
The answer lies not in the delicacy
Or the fragility of its structure.

Its endless strength is the pulse of life,
Strong because it does only one thing.
It grows only in one direction.
Therefore the flower itself needs no strength,
It is only sheltering the life force
Which uncurls like a great wave
With unbelievable momentum,
Only to crash and recede ready to grow again.

I think that is why the naming of wild flowers
Fills me with joy and comfort.
Delicate flowers which rise on that life force
Need not be ugly or harmful.
Though they are short-lived,
They will come again next year.
Somehow if I can name them;
Say their names out loud;
I can borrow some of their energy
And wrap myself in their once-a-year magic.

THESE TEARS,
OR,
UPON THE DEATH OF MY MOTHER

These tears do not bathe my cheeks,
They burn traces indelible.
Imagine.
What if the last words you spoke
Would be the last ones you ever had a chance to say?

My eyes are not washed by these tears.
They are occluded with these acid rivers.
Can words really spawn such polluted tears,
So noxious that they dissolve my flesh on their way
To the dust on these marble floors?

What poison is this that must find its way from my eyes?
Is this the best gift from my mother?
Me, who was propelled from her womb fully two months
before my time;
I, who escaped further damage from her;
Could I know then, before my first breath, that all good had
been absorbed from her in seven months?
That all she could offer me from then on would be only poison?
Poison from alcohol,
Poison from smoke,
But more –
Poison from hate and fear and neurosis?

So, even as a babe, though she tried to teach me differently,
I was born with a wisdom of survival,
And refused what I could of the pain she would have passed on to me.
Passed on, not willingly, or purposefully,
Passed on even as she fought against it,
But passed on to her offspring in spite of all her love.

And yet, now, at her passing, I cannot stop my tears, and these tears burn.
Perhaps it is so because it was always so – ever since my conception.
My mother, poor mother, conceived of her life and her children in tears.
"Mother, oh Mother, please,... let me go."

When I begged her to let me go free, to go on with her business of dying,
Those words were perhaps, the last words she heard me speak.
Even if I could recall them, because I did not want her to die,
Not really,
It would make no difference to her life or her death.

These tears, her tears, my tears, burn from the soul outward,
and no amount of wishing can make them pure and cleansing.
These tears are blood tears.
They come from our marrow – from the fluid of my mother's womb and perhaps her mother's before her.
These tears will never wash away.

I cannot regret them, however.
I only hope that these tears and her suffering will be the
strength for me and for my daughters.
As the world advances, tears that spring from blood and bone
Will be our only connection to the seas of the womb.
They are a true expression of life in its natural cycle.
These tears bring us the wisdom of survival.
Without them we are only pale, wistful apparitions of
humanity
Unbound from the earth.

VESSEL

At the end of the day –
The bottom of the vessel;
When what I hoped
Was planned;
When what was planned
Was not accomplished;
When the morning poured
Into an afternoon with a hole in it–

The hopes and plans
Poured out, gone, lamented,
And impossible to replace,

I end up here
Looking up at the ceiling
At the bottom of the day
And it's too dark at the top.

Too dark to see the cause of the morning's waste,
And how it could have been prevented.
A thumb in the dike might have worked
If only I had seen the breach in time;
The flow of time might have slowed.

I can only hope for a new vessel;
Another look from the top to the bottom;
Another plan, a cork to fill the hole,
And a different vantage point –

So the vessel at the bottom
Is as full as it looked from the top.

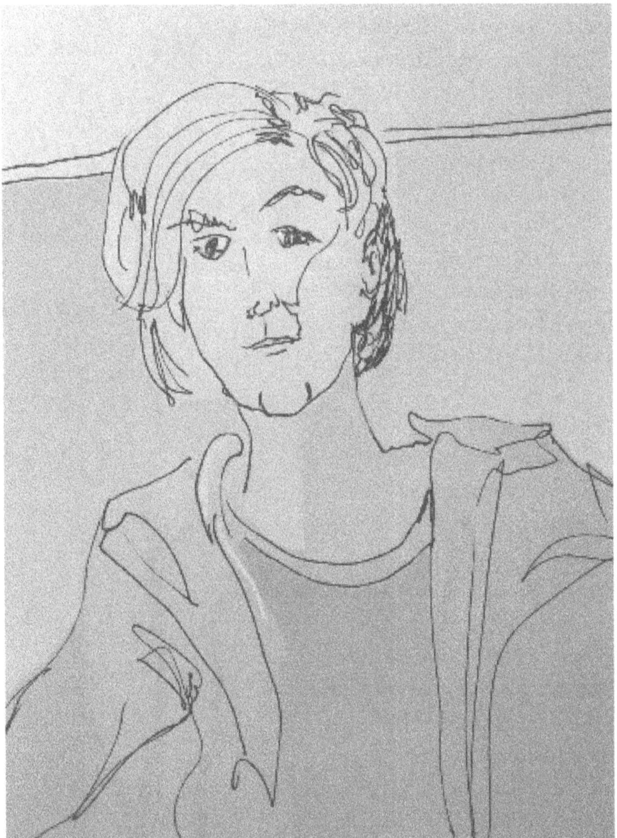

WHEN I WAS YOUNG

When I was young, shop boys
And baggers wore shirts and ties
And obsequious attitudes.
Now? Well, ...what's to tell??
I am proud, ... and not,
That my age can be mistaken,
For I don't leave my house
Without seeing myself
In my 20X mirror
To apply mascara.
I do not leave my house
Without eyebrows.

I refuse to share
My features fading away,
Graying into oblivion.
For I am not fading.
I am full of life and energy!
Though it may not appeal to the young.

Where are you young'uns?
Why let the old wizened men,
Who've surrendered to
The weasling tongues of power,
Run the show?
Raise your sites!
Away from your phones and screens.
Recognize that those screens
Only show you facades.

They only play a shadow show of some
Circus barker's imagination.
Those manufactured images
Are no substitute for life.

They may be entertaining,
And catch your interest for a time,
But ultimately you will only know,
How 'only' you are
In a sea of otherwise-occupied-human- beings.
Easy for me to say, you say,
For I am not immune.
Who is that in the mirror that I worship
Before the door to the outside world,
After my mascara is applied?
Is that not just as alluring an illusion
As the Facebook friend we court?
This two-dimensioned backward face
I hide myself behind?

The natives were right of course
That in the tin type image
The photographer brought forth,
Lay the heart, the seed of someone's soul,
Bare and unprotected from the storm.
And once it's out, the sad news is,
No one can put its life back
Nor change the brittle edge
Left on the skin of paper
Sliced from the heart of a tree.

THE FOREST FOR THE TREES

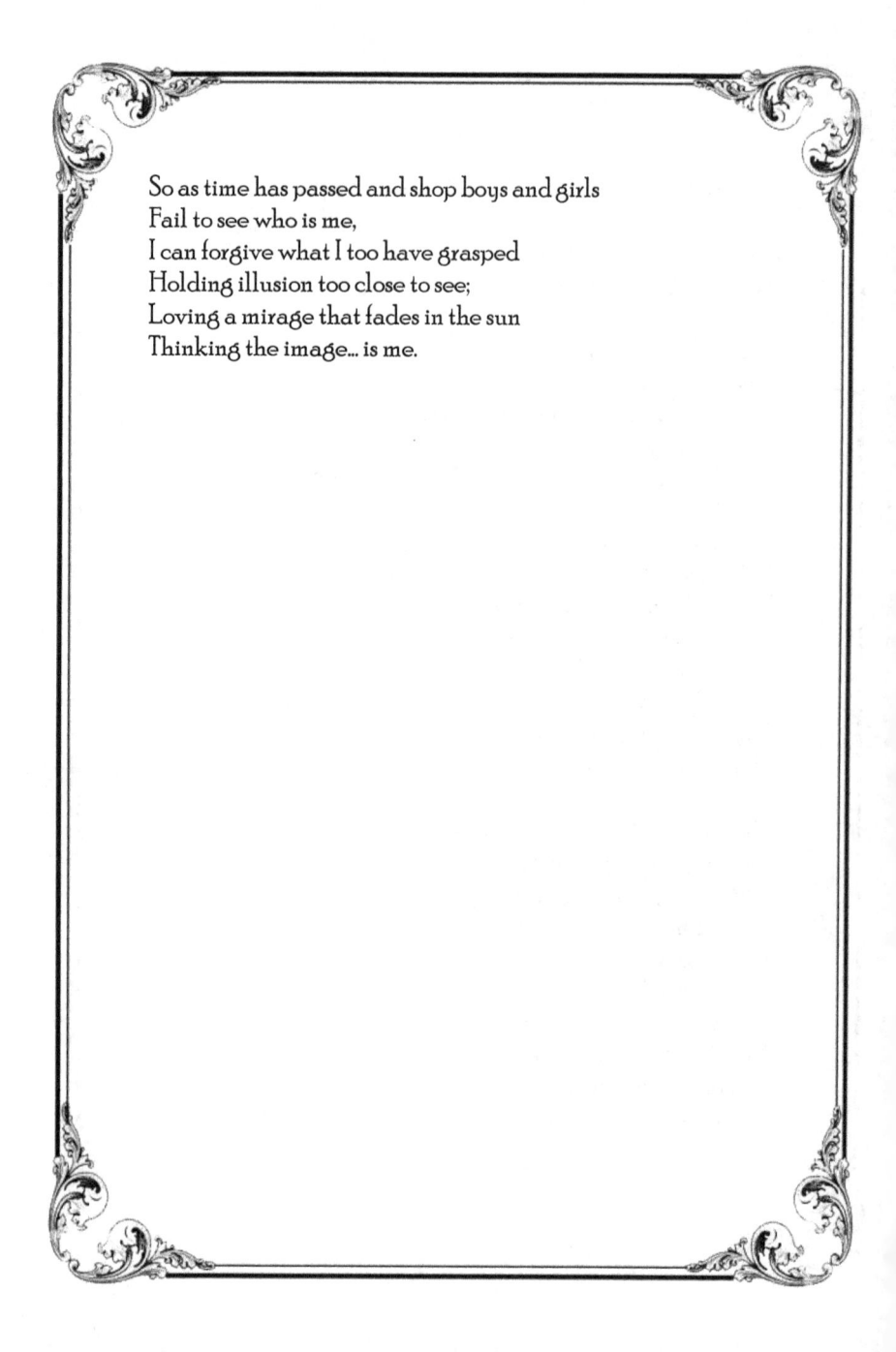

So as time has passed and shop boys and girls
Fail to see who is me,
I can forgive what I too have grasped
Holding illusion too close to see;
Loving a mirage that fades in the sun
Thinking the image... is me.

WHEN POETRY STRIKES

When poetry strikes,
It starts as a rhythm in my head.
As the words arrive,
They come armed with meter and tone.

They are definitely not prose,
And as I hear those newborn words,
The voice ricochets echoing
Until it discovers its final form.

One of the oddest sensations
And you might know this yourself,
Is the feeling
That the poetry voice
Is sort of giving dictation,
As though we don't own the words
At all.

Instead they come down
From some mysterious river
Of... literary music.

Observe it flowing onto the page.
See? We don't create it.
It writes itself,
And we only come back later
...To edit.

THE FOREST FOR THE TREES

The best poetry,
I think, comes from
Something unexpected that
We notice in the natural world,
That we loll around in for a while,
Until appreciation overtakes us.

Share this gift,
Notice some small thing
That in our normal lives we pass by,
And suddenly, these small, unnoticed things
You see and understand,
Are more precious than gold.

The reality is too,
That virtual reproduction
Only captures the real things.
It does not recreate them.
Or really do them justice.
And most certainly,
It does not include us.

So, we need to go for a walk in the woods.
Or, we need to look up at the sky.
For a screen shot
Does just what it sounds like.
And leaves us with the carcass, not the joy.

Better to be struck by poetry,
Than to have our senses slowly dulled
By a laptop or cell phone along the way.

BIRGITTA

Meet Birgitta.
She is very clean.
Cleanliness is next to Godliness.
She doesn't think of herself that way,
But throws herself into the work
Because it is right, and no amount of energy is too much.
Her house is clean inside and out.
Her yard thrives without weeds.
The flowers bloom lavishly with constant good health.
Her herbs are so flavorful that her stews fairly sing.

One lady praises Birgitta saying,
"You can eat off her floors."
Another says, "You could wear white gloves
And never see a speck of dust."
Her silver is polished, her crystal shines.
Her laundry smells of fresh air and sunshine,
The Household gods smile down on her
Her industry is good, and keeps her busy.
There is little time for reflection
Though she could see herself in her countertop
If she had time and inclination to look.

Such a kindly soul with never a bad word for anyone,
If you stop in unexpectedly to chat
She always has a warm cup and a plate of something
delectable for you
And time to sit and share.
Have you met her already? Is she a longtime friend?
I envy you this friendship. She is a rare and priceless gem.

She also has a family of spiders who live happily in her home.
They don't dare descend from the ceilings.
She wouldn't welcome them in.
I am afraid she has no pity for them -
Nature's housewives whose lifelong job it is to keep the earth clean.
They don't speak well of a good housewife in her mind.
Luckily for them, Birgitta's house is clean from the floor to the top of the windows.
From there on, the spiders do the work because
Birgitta never looks up.

THE JOKE

Got carded the other day
An' you've got to know,
I've already passed that mark
Three times in a row!

Three times already...
I had to laugh;
Wanted to tell the young man
Counting my life
On the other side of the conveyor belt,
"Har, Har, Har,
Get it?"

But, I restrained myself.
That joke is wasted on the young.

THE STATUE

I want to meet the sculptor.
Want to look him in the eye;
To see into his heart;
Want to ask him why?

Does he hate the music?
Or maybe just the rhymes?
Does he despise the people?
Or maybe just the times?

I often see his statue,
In fact, I see it every day,
Sitting as it does
In the circle
Its bulk blocking the way.

Terpsichore is dead it seems,
Melody is drowned.
His figures lack in gracefulness,
But genitals abound.
Gestures stiff and lifeless,
Stuck in stone wrapp'd round.

I want to meet the sculptor;
Want to look him in the eye,
For I think he can not help it,
Much as he might try.

For the music can be deadly;
Making money's the reason why,
And it's sex that sells it.
If you think it's something else again,
You've fallen for the lie.

THE FOREST FOR THE TREES

The Poet

Mimi Pantelides

Mimi is a recent resident of Music Row in Nashville, TN. She is a grandmother of three, mother of two, and wife of one. From 1994 until 2014, she lived and taught Centered Riding at their horse farm in Franklin.

For 20 years before moving to Tennessee, Mimi and her family lived in New York just outside of Manhattan. At that time, she danced in a company named "Potpourri" and taught dance, frequently wrote poems and stories, and enjoyed family life with her husband Sokrates and their two girls, Kate and Natasha.

In 1973, Mimi and Sok married, then graduated from the University of Illinois, and moved to San Francisco, California. San Francisco was a wonderful place for newlyweds to live.

Before college and marriage, Mimi lived in rural Illinois. She grew up in a family where classical music played on the radio all day. Her mother was a concert pianist and all 'round artist; her father amused himself after work with rare plantings and architectural drawing. Their home was in horse country. Her life is a continuing spiral of learning to see beauty and share it.

THE FOREST FOR THE TREES

MIMI PANTELIDES

The Producer

Bobby King
Audio Files Producer, Bassist/Guitarist

Bobby King is musician, songwriter, producer and recording engineer. Originally from Philadelphia, PA, he has made Nashville, TN his home since 1991. Bobby is a multi-instrumentalist (bass, guitar, percussion) who has toured and recorded with people like Tanya Tucker, T. Graham Brown, Holly Dunn, John Berry, Donna Ulisse, Martha and the Vandellas, Bo Diddley, The Soul Survivors, and many others. He is active in Nashville's music scene as a studio musician, and has produced many CDs, commercials, and songwriter demos.

THE FOREST FOR THE TREES

The Musician

Will Barrow
Audio Files Keyboards

Will Barrow is a Grammy-winning pianist, singer-songwriter, composer, and multi-instrumentalist whose work reflects the depth and diversity of his life in music. Will has toured and concertized with an eclectic array of artists, including vocalists Gregory Porter, Catherine Russel, and Eloise Laws; instrumentalists Ronnie and Hubert Laws (jazz), singers BeBe Winans, Vickie Sue Robinson, and Freda Payne (R&B); vocalist Suzy Bogguss and Banjoist Alison Brown (Americana); rockers Rosie Flores and Wanda Jackson (rockabilly); and vocalists Crystal Gayle, Steve Wariner, and the Gatlin Brothers. He has been featured on recordings by guitarist Tommy Emmanuel, singer Gilbert O'Sullivan, Gail Davies (along with saxophonist Benny Golson), Ms. Brown (playing on tracks with the Indigo Girls and Colin Hay); operatic soprano Karen Parks, Ms. Bogguss, the Gatlins, and Ms. Flores (for whom he co-produced a CD). Will contributed and instrumental cut to "Beautiful Dreamer, the songs of Stephen Foster", which won a Grammy in 2004. His radio appearances include "A Prairie Home Companion", E-Town, Mountain Stage, and Voice of America; and he's been on TV on BET on Jazz and VH1.

Will has been based in Nashville since 2002 and is a regular in clubs, recording studios, and The Grand Ole Opry. He teaches privately and has taught at the Nashville Jazz Workshop. Before living in Nashville, Will was in New York City for 14 years playing clubs, sessions, tours, and the

Broadway orchestra pits. He received a master's degree from Manhattan School of Music. He has been involved with many musical theatre productions over the years, including two Broadway national touring companies of "A Civil War" (conductor), Gregory Porter's "Nat King Cole and Me", "Low Down Dirty Blues" (featuring Gregory Porter and Tony-nominee Felecia Fields), "Kat and the Kings" (Broadway), "I'll Take You There – The Music of Muscle Shoals" (with Ms. Fields), and "From My Hometown" (an original R&B musical for which he was co-writer).

Will's original music, performances, and recordings reflect the eclectic palate of music with which he's been involved and by with he has been inspired in his nearly 50 years of actively playing and writing music. He has recorded 2 CDs of original songs, "Find A Way" and "State of Grace", featuring stellar Nashville players and his own recording concepts, playing, and singing. His newest project, which he is currently recording and concertizing, is called "Homage", a series of works by Chopin, Beethoven, Ravel, Scriabin re-imaged, along with original instrumentals and songs by Will that are inspired by classical works. These originals and interpretations use grooves from Brazilian music (a world of music of which Will particularly fond), jazz, singer-songwriter styles, and world music. The recording was completed in 2020.